Fuck it
2024 Planner
Sassy Quotes Press

You are fucking amazing

And you need a planner that really gets that. One that's funny, fun to use and will help you get shit done.

Strong women use strong language!
Language that's as creative and colorful as you are and helps you deal with assholes and bullshit.

This planner is filled with motivational swear quotes and affirmations to help you laugh and stay positive as fuck.

You'll also find gratitude prompts and checklists to make sure you're saving your fucks for important shit.

All in a clear, easy-to-use format that will help you stay focused and avoid shitshows.

So drop those f-bombs! Let those fucks fly!
Be your awesome self!

And enjoy the kickass year you deserve.

Starting. Right. Fucking. Now.

Inside your planner

- *2024-2025* Reference calendars
- *2024 Important Dates* by month
- *Goals & Shit* - Goal setting page
- *Shit List* - Hilarious, sweary insults for dealing with assholes
- *January - December 2024* Monthly calendar grids with funny motivational quotes
- *Weekly Planning Pages* with even *more* funny swear word sayings
- Your *Brilliant Thoughts & Shit* notes pages

 *BONUS Gift* - New in 2024, this planner includes a printable set of *48 Sweary Affirmation Cards* in beautiful, watercolor designs! (Instant download link at the back of this planner)

To sign up for more Instant Freebies and Weekly Prize Giveaways visit
SassyQuotesPress.com

Do you have questions? Comments? I would love to hear from you!
Please email Jen@SassyQuotesPress.com

This Belongs to:

_____

_____

_____

_____

_____

2024

January

S	M	T	W	T	F	S
	1	2	3	4	5	6
7	8	9	10	11	12	13
14	15	16	17	18	19	20
21	22	23	24	25	26	27
28	29	30	31			

February

S	M	T	W	T	F	S
				1	2	3
4	5	6	7	8	9	10
11	12	13	14	15	16	17
18	19	20	21	22	23	24
25	26	27	28	29		

March

S	M	T	W	T	F	S
					1	2
3	4	5	6	7	8	9
10	11	12	13	14	15	16
17	18	19	20	21	22	23
24	25	26	27	28	29	30
31						

April

S	M	T	W	T	F	S
	1	2	3	4	5	6
7	8	9	10	11	12	13
14	15	16	17	18	19	20
21	22	23	24	25	26	27
28	29	30				

May

S	M	T	W	T	F	S
			1	2	3	4
5	6	7	8	9	10	11
12	13	14	15	16	17	18
19	20	21	22	23	24	25
26	27	28	29	30	31	

June

S	M	T	W	T	F	S
						1
2	3	4	5	6	7	8
9	10	11	12	13	14	15
16	17	18	19	20	21	22
23	24	25	26	27	28	29
30						

July

S	M	T	W	T	F	S
	1	2	3	4	5	6
7	8	9	10	11	12	13
14	15	16	17	18	19	20
21	22	23	24	25	26	27
28	29	30	31			

August

S	M	T	W	T	F	S
				1	2	3
4	5	6	7	8	9	10
11	12	13	14	15	16	17
18	19	20	21	22	23	24
25	26	27	28	29	30	31

September

S	M	T	W	T	F	S
1	2	3	4	5	6	7
8	9	10	11	12	13	14
15	16	17	18	19	20	21
22	23	24	25	26	27	28
29	30					

October

S	M	T	W	T	F	S
	1	2	3	4	5
6	7	8	9	10	11	12
13	14	15	16	17	18	19
20	21	22	23	24	25	26
27	28	29	30	31		

November

S	M	T	W	T	F	S
					1	2
3	4	5	6	7	8	9
10	11	12	13	14	15	16
17	18	19	20	21	22	23
24	25	26	27	28	29	30

December

S	M	T	W	T	F	S
1	2	3	4	5	6	7
8	9	10	11	12	13	14
15	16	17	18	19	20	21
22	23	24	25	26	27	28
29	30	31				

2025

January

S	M	T	W	T	F	S
			1	2	3	4
5	6	7	8	9	10	11
12	13	14	15	16	17	18
19	20	21	22	23	24	25
26	27	28	29	30	31	

February

S	M	T	W	T	F	S
						1
2	3	4	5	6	7	8
9	10	11	12	13	14	15
16	17	18	19	20	21	22
23	24	25	26	27	28	

March

S	M	T	W	T	F	S
						1
2	3	4	5	6	7	8
9	10	11	12	13	14	15
16	17	18	19	20	21	22
23	24	25	26	27	28	29
30	31					

April

S	M	T	W	T	F	S
		1	2	3	4	5
6	7	8	9	10	11	12
13	14	15	16	17	18	19
20	21	22	23	24	25	26
27	28	29	30			

May

S	M	T	W	T	F	S
				1	2	3
4	5	6	7	8	9	10
11	12	13	14	15	16	17
18	19	20	21	22	23	24
25	26	27	28	29	30	31

June

S	M	T	W	T	F	S
1	2	3	4	5	6	7
8	9	10	11	12	13	14
15	16	17	18	19	20	21
22	23	24	25	26	27	28
29	30					

July

S	M	T	W	T	F	S
		1	2	3	4	5
6	7	8	9	10	11	12
13	14	15	16	17	18	19
20	21	22	23	24	25	26
27	28	29	30	31		

August

S	M	T	W	T	F	S
					1	2
3	4	5	6	7	8	9
10	11	12	13	14	15	16
17	18	19	20	21	22	23
24	25	26	27	28	29	30
31						

September

S	M	T	W	T	F	S
	1	2	3	4	5	6
7	8	9	10	11	12	13
14	15	16	17	18	19	20
21	22	23	24	25	26	27
28	29	30				

October

S	M	T	W	T	F	S
			1	2	3	4
5	6	7	8	9	10	11
12	13	14	15	16	17	18
19	20	21	22	23	24	25
26	27	28	29	30	31	

November

S	M	T	W	T	F	S
						1
2	3	4	5	6	7	8
9	10	11	12	13	14	15
16	17	18	19	20	21	22
23	24	25	26	27	28	29
30						

December

S	M	T	W	T	F	S
	1	2	3	4	5	6
7	8	9	10	11	12	13
14	15	16	17	18	19	20
21	22	23	24	25	26	27
28	29	30	31			

2024 Important Dates

JANUARY

FEBRUARY

MAY

JUNE

SEPTEMBER

OCTOBER

2024 Important Dates

MARCH

APRIL

JULY

AUGUST

NOVEMBER

DECEMBER

You are an amazing human.
You have an awesome ability to learn and grow.
You will always be worthy of love.

Thanks for coming to my TED Talk, bitch

Goals & Shit

What goals do you want to crush with your awesomeness? Self care, relationships, hobbies, work? Your possibilities are endless.

_____
_____
_____
_____
_____
_____
_____
_____
_____
_____
_____
_____
_____
_____
_____
_____
_____
_____
_____
_____
_____
_____
_____
_____
_____
_____
_____
_____
_____

Shit List

You don't have time for assholes! With this handy list of insults and comebacks, you can clap back and keep fucking going.

- Nice. You've got that asshole-hair-don't care vibe going on.
- You'd be great on that new show... The Great American Fuckoff.
- Do you use regular toilet paper? Or do you have to buy special bullshit wipes for your mouth?
- I wouldn't call you a huge asshole. I prefer anally gifted.
- You spark sadness. And nobody wants a used asshole, so kindly Kondo yourself into the trash.
- Fuck-ups aren't like push-ups. Your goal shouldn't be doing as many as you can.
- Damn it. I put my phone on Do Not Disturb, but you're still here.
- You're proof that AI isn't a big deal. You've been faking intelligence your whole life.
- Let me guess. You grew up in Whatthefuckville.
- You're not a total asshole. You're at least 30% shithead.
- You can't act like an asshole and think people will still like you. You're not a cat.
- If it walks like a dick and talks like a dick, it's probably a you.
- I've got a great deal for you. Get 10 fuck offs the asshole special just for shutting up.
- A dumbass like you could only have graduated from Fuck U.
- I think your fucking brain has stopped working. Have you tried turning it off and turning it on again?
- Good news. Size does matter and you are an enormous dick.
- Living with intention is good. But why did you intend to be an asshole?
- I just want you to be happy. And the key to happiness is getting the fuck away from me.
- Your face is truly epic. We're talking "launch a thousand shits" epic.
- Your hormones must be out of whack. If you want them whacked back into place, I'd love to help.
- Giving 110% is great. But not when it comes to being an asshole.
- This is an asshole-free zone. I'm going to have to ask you to back up. Preferably down a flight of stairs.
- Tourists must love taking pictures with you. "Look at me, standing next to the World's Biggest Asshole!"
- No offense, butt. That's it. That's the insult.

December 2023

Go home 2023! You're drunk.

28 THURSDAY

29 FRIDAY

30 SATURDAY

○
○
○
○

31 SUNDAY

New Year's Eve

○
○
○
○
○
○
○
○
○

○
○
○
○
○
○
○
○
○

○
○
○
○

Notes and shit

January 2024

Sunday	Monday	Tuesday	Wednesday
	1 New Year's Day	2	3
7	8	9	10
14	15 Martin Luther King Jr. Day (US)	16	17
21	22	23	24
28	29	30	31

Welcome 2024: Year of the Badass

Thursday	Friday	Saturday	Important shit
4	5	6	_____
			_____
11	12	13	_____
			_____
18	19	20	_____
			_____
25	26	27	_____
			_____

December 2023

S	M	T	W	T	F	S
					1	2
3	4	5	6	7	8	9
10	11	12	13	14	15	16
17	18	19	20	21	22	23
24	25	26	27	28	29	30
31						

February 2024

S	M	T	W	T	F	S
				1	2	3
4	5	6	7	8	9	10
11	12	13	14	15	16	17
18	19	20	21	22	23	24
25	26	27	28	29		

January 2024

○
○
○
○
○
○
○
○
○

○
○
○
○
○
○
○
○
○

○
○
○
○
○
○
○
○
○

Important as fuck

Fucking grateful for...

Happy Fucking New Year!

4 THURSDAY

_____
_____
_____
_____
_____
_____
_____
_____
_____
_____
_____
_____
_____
_____
_____
_____
_____
_____

- ○ _____
- ○ _____
- ○ _____
- ○ _____
- ○ _____
- ○ _____
- ○ _____
- ○ _____
- ○ _____

5 FRIDAY

_____
_____
_____
_____
_____
_____
_____
_____
_____
_____
_____
_____
_____
_____
_____
_____
_____
_____

- ○ _____
- ○ _____
- ○ _____
- ○ _____
- ○ _____
- ○ _____
- ○ _____
- ○ _____
- ○ _____

6 SATURDAY

_____
_____
_____
_____
_____
_____
- ○ _____
- ○ _____
- ○ _____
- ○ _____

7 SUNDAY

_____
_____
_____
_____
_____
_____
- ○ _____
- ○ _____
- ○ _____
- ○ _____

Notes and shit

_____
_____
_____

January 2024

Important as fuck

Fucking grateful for...

live, laugh, love... shop, exercise, do laundry, grab drinks, watch a movie... are all things you can write on planning pages like this. Go fuckin' nuts.

11 THURSDAY   **12 FRIDAY**   **13 SATURDAY**

_____   _____   _____
_____   _____   _____
_____   _____   _____
_____   _____   _____
_____   _____   _____
_____   _____   _____
_____   _____   ○ _____
_____   _____   ○ _____
_____   _____   ○ _____
_____   _____   ○ _____
_____   _____

_____   _____   **14 SUNDAY**

_____   _____   _____
_____   _____   _____
_____   _____   _____
_____   _____   _____
_____   _____   _____
○ _____   ○ _____   _____
○ _____   ○ _____   _____
○ _____   ○ _____   _____
○ _____   ○ _____   _____
○ _____   ○ _____
○ _____   ○ _____   ○ _____
○ _____   ○ _____   ○ _____
○ _____   ○ _____   ○ _____
○ _____   ○ _____   ○ _____

Notes and shit

_____
_____
_____

January 2024

15 MONDAY

Martin Luther King Jr. Day (US)

16 TUESDAY

17 WEDNESDAY

Important as fuck

Fucking grateful for...

You are fucking beautiful, inside and out

18 THURSDAY

19 FRIDAY

20 SATURDAY

○
○
○
○

21 SUNDAY

○
○
○
○
○
○
○
○
○

○
○
○
○
○
○
○
○
○

○
○
○
○

Notes and shit

January 2024

○
○
○
○
○
○
○
○
○

Important as fuck

Fucking grateful for...

You did not wake up today to follow assholes

25 THURSDAY

_____
_____
_____
_____
_____
_____
_____
_____
_____
_____
_____
_____
_____
_____
_____

○ _____
○ _____
○ _____
○ _____
○ _____
○ _____
○ _____
○ _____
○ _____

26 FRIDAY

_____
_____
_____
_____
_____
_____
_____
_____
_____
_____
_____
_____
_____
_____
_____

○ _____
○ _____
○ _____
○ _____
○ _____
○ _____
○ _____
○ _____
○ _____

27 SATURDAY

_____
_____
_____
_____
_____
○ _____
○ _____
○ _____
○ _____

28 SUNDAY

_____
_____
_____
_____
_____
○ _____
○ _____
○ _____
○ _____

Notes and shit

_____
_____
_____

January-February 2024

29 MONDAY **30 TUESDAY** **31 WEDNESDAY**

Important as fuck

Fucking grateful for...

You could teach a badass masterclass

1 THURSDAY

_____
_____
_____
_____
_____
_____
_____
_____
_____
_____
_____
_____
_____
_____
_____
_____
_____

○ _____
○ _____
○ _____
○ _____
○ _____
○ _____
○ _____
○ _____
○ _____

2 FRIDAY

_____
_____
_____
_____
_____
_____
_____
_____
_____
_____
_____
_____
_____
_____

○ _____
○ _____
○ _____
○ _____
○ _____
○ _____
○ _____
○ _____
○ _____

3 SATURDAY

_____
_____
_____
_____
_____
_____
○ _____
○ _____
○ _____
○ _____

4 SUNDAY

_____
_____
_____
_____
_____
_____
_____
○ _____
○ _____
○ _____
○ _____

Notes and shit

_____
_____
_____

February 2024

Sunday	Monday	Tuesday	Wednesday
4	5	6	7
11	12	13	14 Ash Wednesday, Valentine's Day
18	19 Presidents' Day (US)	20	21
25	26	27	28

You are a fucking delight

Thursday	Friday	Saturday
1	2	3
8	9	10 Chinese New Year, Lunar New Year
15	16	17
22	23	24
29 Leap Day		

Important shit

_____
_____
_____
_____
_____
_____
_____
_____
_____
_____
_____
_____
_____
_____
_____
_____
_____
_____
_____
_____
_____
_____
_____
_____
_____
_____
_____

January 2024

S	M	T	W	T	F	S
	1	2	3	4	5	6
7	8	9	10	11	12	13
14	15	16	17	18	19	20
21	22	23	24	25	26	27
28	29	30	31			

March 2024

S	M	T	W	T	F	S
					1	2
3	4	5	6	7	8	9
10	11	12	13	14	15	16
17	18	19	20	21	22	23
24	25	26	27	28	29	30
31						

February 2024

Important as fuck

Fucking grateful for...

Remember your Why so you can power through your What the Fucks?!

8 THURSDAY

9 FRIDAY

10 SATURDAY

Chinese New Year, Lunar New Year

- ○
- ○
- ○
- ○

11 SUNDAY

8 THURSDAY
- ○
- ○
- ○
- ○
- ○
- ○
- ○
- ○
- ○

9 FRIDAY
- ○
- ○
- ○
- ○
- ○
- ○
- ○
- ○
- ○

11 SUNDAY
- ○
- ○
- ○
- ○

Notes and shit

February 2024

12 MONDAY

13 TUESDAY

14 WEDNESDAY

Ash Wednesday, Valentine's Day

Important as fuck

Fucking grateful for...

Happy Yucky Tasting Candy Hearts Day to all who celebrate

15 THURSDAY

_____
_____
_____
_____
_____
_____
_____
_____
_____
_____
_____
_____
_____
_____
_____
_____
_____
○ _____
○ _____
○ _____
○ _____
○ _____
○ _____
○ _____
○ _____
○ _____

16 FRIDAY

_____
_____
_____
_____
_____
_____
_____
_____
_____
_____
_____
_____
_____
_____
_____
_____
_____
○ _____
○ _____
○ _____
○ _____
○ _____
○ _____
○ _____
○ _____
○ _____

17 SATURDAY

_____
_____
_____
_____
_____
○ _____
○ _____
○ _____
○ _____

18 SUNDAY

_____
_____
_____
_____
_____
_____
○ _____
○ _____
○ _____
○ _____

Notes and shit

_____
_____
_____

February 2024

19 MONDAY

Presidents' Day (US)

_____
_____
_____
_____
_____
_____
_____
_____
_____
_____
_____
_____
_____
_____
_____
_____
_____
_____
_____

- ○ _____
- ○ _____
- ○ _____
- ○ _____
- ○ _____
- ○ _____
- ○ _____
- ○ _____
- ○ _____

20 TUESDAY

_____
_____
_____
_____
_____
_____
_____
_____
_____
_____
_____
_____
_____
_____
_____
_____
_____
_____
_____

- ○ _____
- ○ _____
- ○ _____
- ○ _____
- ○ _____
- ○ _____
- ○ _____
- ○ _____
- ○ _____

21 WEDNESDAY

_____
_____
_____
_____
_____
_____
_____
_____
_____
_____
_____
_____
_____
_____
_____
_____
_____
_____
_____

- ○ _____
- ○ _____
- ○ _____
- ○ _____
- ○ _____
- ○ _____
- ○ _____
- ○ _____
- ○ _____

Important as fuck

_____
_____
_____

Fucking grateful for...

_____
_____
_____

Think big. Start small. Keep fucking going.

22 THURSDAY

_____
_____
_____
_____
_____
_____
_____
_____
_____
_____
_____
_____
_____
_____
_____

○ _____
○ _____
○ _____
○ _____
○ _____
○ _____
○ _____
○ _____
○ _____

23 FRIDAY

_____
_____
_____
_____
_____
_____
_____
_____
_____
_____
_____
_____
_____
_____
_____

○ _____
○ _____
○ _____
○ _____
○ _____
○ _____
○ _____
○ _____
○ _____

24 SATURDAY

_____
_____
_____
_____
_____

○ _____
○ _____
○ _____
○ _____

25 SUNDAY

_____
_____
_____
_____
_____

○ _____
○ _____
○ _____
○ _____

Notes and shit

_____
_____

February-March 2024

26 MONDAY   **27 TUESDAY**   **28 WEDNESDAY**

Important as fuck

Fucking grateful for...

Happy Fucking Leap Year! The world gets an extra day of your awesomeness.

29 THURSDAY
Leap Day

_____
_____
_____
_____
_____
_____
_____
_____
_____
_____
_____
_____
_____
_____
_____
_____
_____

○ _____
○ _____
○ _____
○ _____
○ _____
○ _____
○ _____
○ _____
○ _____

1 FRIDAY

_____
_____
_____
_____
_____
_____
_____
_____
_____
_____
_____
_____
_____
_____

○ _____
○ _____
○ _____
○ _____
○ _____
○ _____
○ _____
○ _____
○ _____

2 SATURDAY

_____
_____
_____
_____
_____
○ _____
○ _____
○ _____
○ _____

3 SUNDAY

_____
_____
_____
_____
_____
_____
_____
○ _____
○ _____
○ _____
○ _____

Notes and shit

_____
_____
_____

March 2024

Sunday	Monday	Tuesday	Wednesday
3	4	5	6
10 Mother's Day (UK) Daylight Saving Time begins (US, CA)	11 First Day of Ramadan begins at sundown	12	13
17 St. Patrick's Day	18	19 Spring begins	20
24 Palm Sunday, Purim begins at sundown	25	26	27
31 Easter Sunday, Dalight Saving Time begins (UK)			

It's shenanigans time, bitches

Thursday	Friday	Saturday	Important shit
	1	2	_____
			_____
			_____
			_____
7	8	9	_____
			_____
			_____
			_____
14	15	16	_____
			_____
			_____
			_____
21	22	23	_____
			_____
			_____
			_____
28	29	30	_____
	Good Friday		_____

February 2024

S	M	T	W	T	F	S
				1	2	3
4	5	6	7	8	9	10
11	12	13	14	15	16	17
18	19	20	21	22	23	24
25	26	27	28	29		

April 2024

S	M	T	W	T	F	S
	1	2	3	4	5	6
7	8	9	10	11	12	13
14	15	16	17	18	19	20
21	22	23	24	25	26	27
28	29	30				

March 2024

4 MONDAY

5 TUESDAY

6 WEDNESDAY

○
○
○
○
○
○
○
○
○

○
○
○
○
○
○
○
○
○

○
○
○
○
○
○
○
○
○

Important as fuck

Fucking grateful for...

No need to change the clocks. It's always Fucks Saving Time.

7 THURSDAY	**8 FRIDAY**	**9 SATURDAY**
_____	_____	_____
_____	_____	_____
_____	_____	_____
_____	_____	_____
_____	_____	_____
_____	_____	_____
_____	_____	○ _____
_____	_____	○ _____
_____	_____	○ _____
_____	_____	○ _____

10 SUNDAY
Daylight Saving Time begins (US, CA),
Mother's Day (UK)

○
○
○
○
○
○
○
○
○

Notes and shit

_____

_____

_____

March 2024

11 MONDAY

First Day of Ramadan begins at sundown

12 TUESDAY

13 WEDNESDAY

○ _____
○ _____
○ _____
○ _____
○ _____
○ _____
○ _____
○ _____
○ _____

○ _____
○ _____
○ _____
○ _____
○ _____
○ _____
○ _____
○ _____
○ _____

○ _____
○ _____
○ _____
○ _____
○ _____
○ _____
○ _____
○ _____
○ _____

Important as fuck

Fucking grateful for...

If St. Patrick can drive the snakes out of Ireland, you can drive the assholes out of your social media feed.

14 THURSDAY

15 FRIDAY

16 SATURDAY

17 SUNDAY

St. Patrick's Day

Notes and shit

March 2024

18 MONDAY

19 TUESDAY

Spring begins

20 WEDNESDAY

○
○
○
○
○
○
○
○
○

○
○
○
○
○
○
○
○
○

○
○
○
○
○
○
○
○
○

Important as fuck

Fucking grateful for...

look on the fucking bright side

21 THURSDAY

_____
_____
_____
_____
_____
_____
_____
_____
_____
_____
_____
_____
_____
_____
_____
_____
○ _____
○ _____
○ _____
○ _____
○ _____
○ _____
○ _____
○ _____
○ _____

22 FRIDAY

_____
_____
_____
_____
_____
_____
_____
_____
_____
_____
_____
_____
_____
_____
_____
_____
○ _____
○ _____
○ _____
○ _____
○ _____
○ _____
○ _____
○ _____
○ _____

23 SATURDAY

_____
_____
_____
_____
_____
_____
○ _____
○ _____
○ _____
○ _____

24 SUNDAY
Palm Sunday, Purim
begins at sundown

_____
_____
_____
_____
_____
_____
_____
_____
○ _____
○ _____
○ _____
○ _____

Notes and shit

_____
_____
_____

March 2024

Important as fuck

Fucking grateful for...

Take the road less traveled, bitch. And your phone. And snacks, of course.

28 THURSDAY

_____
_____
_____
_____
_____
_____
_____
_____
_____
_____
_____
_____
_____
_____
_____
_____
_____
○ _____
○ _____
○ _____
○ _____
○ _____
○ _____
○ _____
○ _____
○ _____

29 FRIDAY
Good Friday

_____
_____
_____
_____
_____
_____
_____
_____
_____
_____
_____
_____
_____
_____
_____
_____
○ _____
○ _____
○ _____
○ _____
○ _____
○ _____
○ _____
○ _____
○ _____

30 SATURDAY

_____
_____
_____
_____
_____
○ _____
○ _____
○ _____
○ _____

31 SUNDAY
Easter Sunday, Daylight
Saving Time begins (UK)

_____
_____
_____
_____
○ _____
○ _____
○ _____
○ _____

Notes and shit

_____
_____
_____

April 2024

Sunday	Monday	Tuesday	Wednesday
	1 April Fool's Day (US), Easter Monday	2	3
7	8	9	10 Eid al-Fitr begins at sundown
14	15	16	17
21	22 Passover begins at sundown, Earth Day (US)	23 St. George's Day (UK)	24
28	29	30	

Heads up. More Mondays than Fridays in this extra bitch.

Thursday	Friday	Saturday	Important shit
4	5	6	_____
11	12	13	_____
18	19	20	_____
25	26	27	_____

March 2024

S	M	T	W	T	F	S
					1	2
3	4	5	6	7	8	9
10	11	12	13	14	15	16
17	18	19	20	21	22	23
24	25	26	27	28	29	30
31						

May 2024

S	M	T	W	T	F	S
			1	2	3	4
5	6	7	8	9	10	11
12	13	14	15	16	17	18
19	20	21	22	23	24	25
26	27	28	29	30	31	

April 2024

○
○
○
○
○
○
○
○
○

○
○
○
○
○
○
○
○
○

○
○
○
○
○
○
○
○
○

Important as fuck

Fucking grateful for...

You: I will make this month my bitch. April: As you wish, Your Hotness.

4 THURSDAY

○ ___
○ ___
○ ___
○ ___
○ ___
○ ___
○ ___
○ ___
○ ___

5 FRIDAY

○ ___
○ ___
○ ___
○ ___
○ ___
○ ___
○ ___
○ ___
○ ___

6 SATURDAY

○ ___
○ ___
○ ___
○ ___

7 SUNDAY

○ ___
○ ___
○ ___
○ ___

Notes and shit

April 2024

8 MONDAY

9 TUESDAY

10 WEDNESDAY

Eid al-Fitr begins at sundown

Important as fuck

Fucking grateful for...

World Asshole Awareness Day is everyday, unfortunately

11 THURSDAY

_____
_____
_____
_____
_____
_____
_____
_____
_____
_____
_____
_____
_____
_____
_____
_____

○ _____
○ _____
○ _____
○ _____
○ _____
○ _____
○ _____
○ _____
○ _____

12 FRIDAY

_____
_____
_____
_____
_____
_____
_____
_____
_____
_____
_____
_____
_____
_____
_____
_____

○ _____
○ _____
○ _____
○ _____
○ _____
○ _____
○ _____
○ _____
○ _____

13 SATURDAY

_____
_____
_____
_____
_____

○ _____
○ _____
○ _____
○ _____

14 SUNDAY

_____
_____
_____
_____
_____
_____
_____
_____

○ _____
○ _____
○ _____
○ _____

Notes and shit

_____
_____
_____

April 2024

Important as fuck

Fucking grateful for...

Today's forecast: 100% chance of bullshit, 0% chance of giving a fuck.

18 THURSDAY   **19 FRIDAY**   **20 SATURDAY**

○
○
○
○

21 SUNDAY

○
○
○
○
○
○   ○
○   ○   ○
○   ○   ○
○   ○   ○

Notes and shit

April 2024

22 MONDAY
Passover begins at sundown,
Earth Day (US)

23 TUESDAY
St. George's Day (UK)

24 WEDNESDAY

Important as fuck

Fucking grateful for...

Assholes are no match for your smokey eye, side eye combo

25 THURSDAY

_____
_____
_____
_____
_____
_____
_____
_____
_____
_____
_____
_____
_____

O _____
O _____
O _____
O _____
O _____
O _____
O _____
O _____
O _____

26 FRIDAY

_____
_____
_____
_____
_____
_____
_____
_____
_____
_____
_____
_____
_____

O _____
O _____
O _____
O _____
O _____
O _____
O _____
O _____
O _____

27 SATURDAY

_____
_____
_____
_____
_____
_____

O _____
O _____
O _____
O _____

28 SUNDAY

_____
_____
_____
_____
_____
_____

O _____
O _____
O _____
O _____

Notes and shit

_____
_____
_____

May 2024

Sunday	Monday	Tuesday	Wednesday
			1
5 Cinco de Mayo (US)	6 Early May Bank Holiday (UK)	7	8
12 Mother's Day (US, CA)	13	14	15
19	20 Victoria Day (CA)	21	22
26	27 Memorial Day (US), Spring Bank Holiday (UK)	28	29

Invest in yourself. Think of it as Bitchcoin.

Thursday	Friday	Saturday	Important shit
2	3	4	_____
9	10	11	_____
16	17	18	_____
23	24	25	_____
30	31		_____

April 2024

S	M	T	W	T	F	S
	1	2	3	4	5	6
7	8	9	10	11	12	13
14	15	16	17	18	19	20
21	22	23	24	25	26	27
28	29	30				

June 2024

S	M	T	W	T	F	S
						1
2	3	4	5	6	7	8
9	10	11	12	13	14	15
16	17	18	19	20	21	22
23	24	25	26	27	28	29
30						

April-May 2024

29 MONDAY   **30 TUESDAY**   **1 WEDNESDAY**

Important as fuck

Fucking grateful for...

Awesome friends are badass and badass friends are awesome

2 THURSDAY

_____
_____
_____
_____
_____
_____
_____
_____
_____
_____
_____
_____
_____
_____
_____
_____
_____
_____

○ _____
○ _____
○ _____
○ _____
○ _____
○ _____
○ _____
○ _____
○ _____

3 FRIDAY

_____
_____
_____
_____
_____
_____
_____
_____
_____
_____
_____
_____
_____
_____
_____
_____
_____
_____

○ _____
○ _____
○ _____
○ _____
○ _____
○ _____
○ _____
○ _____
○ _____

4 SATURDAY

_____
_____
_____
_____
_____
_____
○ _____
○ _____
○ _____
○ _____

5 SUNDAY
Cinco de Mayo (US)

_____
_____
_____
_____
_____
_____
○ _____
○ _____
○ _____
○ _____

Notes and shit

_____
_____
_____

May 2024

6 MONDAY

Early May Bank Holiday (UK)

7 TUESDAY

8 WEDNESDAY

○
○
○
○
○
○
○
○
○

○
○
○
○
○
○
○
○
○

○
○
○
○
○
○
○
○
○

Important as fuck

Fucking grateful for...

Cringe attack survival tip: let that shit go

9 THURSDAY

_____
_____
_____
_____
_____
_____
_____
_____
_____
_____
_____
_____
_____
_____
_____
_____
○ _____
○ _____
○ _____
○ _____
○ _____
○ _____
○ _____
○ _____
○ _____

10 FRIDAY

_____
_____
_____
_____
_____
_____
_____
_____
_____
_____
_____
_____
_____
_____
_____
_____
○ _____
○ _____
○ _____
○ _____
○ _____
○ _____
○ _____
○ _____
○ _____

11 SATURDAY

_____
_____
_____
_____
_____
_____
_____
○ _____
○ _____
○ _____
○ _____

12 SUNDAY
Mother's Day (US, CA)

_____
_____
_____
_____
_____
○ _____
○ _____
○ _____
○ _____

Notes and shit

_____
_____
_____

May 2024

13 MONDAY

14 TUESDAY

15 WEDNESDAY

Important as fuck

Fucking grateful for...

Boss Bitch is a good look for you

16 THURSDAY

_____
_____
_____
_____
_____
_____
_____
_____
_____
_____
_____
_____
_____
_____
_____
_____

○ _____
○ _____
○ _____
○ _____
○ _____
○ _____
○ _____
○ _____
○ _____

17 FRIDAY

_____
_____
_____
_____
_____
_____
_____
_____
_____
_____
_____
_____
_____
_____
_____
_____

○ _____
○ _____
○ _____
○ _____
○ _____
○ _____
○ _____
○ _____
○ _____

18 SATURDAY

_____
_____
_____
_____
_____
_____

○ _____
○ _____
○ _____
○ _____

19 SUNDAY

_____
_____
_____
_____
_____
_____

○ _____
○ _____
○ _____
○ _____

Notes and shit

_____
_____
_____

May 2024

20 MONDAY

Victoria Day (CA)

21 TUESDAY

22 WEDNESDAY

○
○
○
○
○
○
○
○
○

○
○
○
○
○
○
○
○
○

○
○
○
○
○
○
○
○
○

Important as fuck

Fucking grateful for...

Did you know that the average person says 80 swear words a day. Fuckin' amateurs.

23 THURSDAY

_____
_____
_____
_____
_____
_____
_____
_____
_____
_____
_____
_____
_____
_____
_____
_____

○ _____
○ _____
○ _____
○ _____
○ _____
○ _____
○ _____
○ _____
○ _____

24 FRIDAY

_____
_____
_____
_____
_____
_____
_____
_____
_____
_____
_____
_____
_____
_____

○ _____
○ _____
○ _____
○ _____
○ _____
○ _____
○ _____
○ _____
○ _____

25 SATURDAY

_____
_____
_____
_____
_____
_____
○ _____
○ _____
○ _____
○ _____

26 SUNDAY

_____
_____
_____
_____
_____
_____
○ _____
○ _____
○ _____
○ _____

Notes and shit

_____
_____
_____

May-June 2024

27 MONDAY
Memorial Day (US), Spring Bank
Holiday (UK)

28 TUESDAY

29 WEDNESDAY

_____
_____
_____
_____
_____
_____
_____
_____
_____
_____
_____
_____
_____
_____
_____
_____

○ _____
○ _____
○ _____
○ _____
○ _____
○ _____
○ _____
○ _____
○ _____

Important as fuck

_____
_____
_____

Fucking grateful for...

_____
_____
_____

Don't take any shit. Take naps, walks and stuff you need. But don't take any shit.

30 THURSDAY

_____
_____
_____
_____
_____
_____
_____
_____
_____
_____
_____
_____
_____
_____
_____
_____

○ _____
○ _____
○ _____
○ _____
○ _____
○ _____
○ _____
○ _____
○ _____

31 FRIDAY

_____
_____
_____
_____
_____
_____
_____
_____
_____
_____
_____
_____
_____
_____
_____
_____

○ _____
○ _____
○ _____
○ _____
○ _____
○ _____
○ _____
○ _____
○ _____

1 SATURDAY

_____
_____
_____
_____
_____
_____
○ _____
○ _____
○ _____
○ _____

2 SUNDAY

_____
_____
_____
_____
_____
_____
_____
○ _____
○ _____
○ _____
○ _____

Notes and shit

_____
_____
_____

June 2024

Sunday	Monday	Tuesday	Wednesday
2	3	4	5
9	10	11	12
16 Father's Day	17	18	19 Juneteenth (US)
23	24	25	26
30			

Bloom bitch

Thursday	Friday	Saturday	Important shit
		1	_____ _____ _____ _____
6	7	8	_____ _____ _____ _____
13	14 Flag Day (US)	15 King's Birthday (UK)	_____ _____ _____ _____
20 Summer begins	21	22	_____ _____ _____ _____
27	28	29	_____ _____ _____ _____

May 2024

S	M	T	W	T	F	S
			1	2	3	4
5	6	7	8	9	10	11
12	13	14	15	16	17	18
19	20	21	22	23	24	25
26	27	28	29	30	31	

July 2024

S	M	T	W	T	F	S
	1	2	3	4	5	6
7	8	9	10	11	12	13
14	15	16	17	18	19	20
21	22	23	24	25	26	27
28	29	30	31			

June 2024

3 MONDAY **4 TUESDAY** **5 WEDNESDAY**

- O
- O
- O
- O
- O
- O
- O
- O
- O

Important as fuck

Fucking grateful for...

"Fuck it" is the "aloha" of swearing. It can mean "Fuck no," "Fuck yes," or whatever the fuck you want it to mean.

6 THURSDAY

7 FRIDAY

8 SATURDAY

○
○
○
○

9 SUNDAY

○
○
○
○
○
○
○
○
○

○
○
○
○
○
○
○
○
○

○
○
○
○

Notes and shit

June 2024

Important as fuck

Fucking grateful for...

It's a beautiful day to get shit done

13 THURSDAY

_____
_____
_____
_____
_____
_____
_____
_____
_____
_____
_____
_____
_____
_____
_____
_____

○ _____
○ _____
○ _____
○ _____
○ _____
○ _____
○ _____
○ _____
○ _____

14 FRIDAY
Flag Day (US)

_____
_____
_____
_____
_____
_____
_____
_____
_____
_____
_____
_____
_____

○ _____
○ _____
○ _____
○ _____
○ _____
○ _____
○ _____
○ _____
○ _____

15 SATURDAY
King's Birthday (UK)

_____
_____
_____
_____
_____
_____

○ _____
○ _____
○ _____
○ _____

16 SUNDAY
Father's Day

_____
_____
_____
_____
_____
_____

○ _____
○ _____
○ _____
○ _____

Notes and shit

_____
_____
_____

June 2024

17 MONDAY

18 TUESDAY

19 WEDNESDAY

Juneteenth (US)

○
○
○
○
○
○
○
○
○

○
○
○
○
○
○
○
○
○

○
○
○
○
○
○
○
○
○

Important as fuck

Fucking grateful for...

What's your beauty secret? Drink water and glow like fucking sunshine?

20 THURSDAY
Summer begins

_____
_____
_____
_____
_____
_____
_____
_____
_____
_____
_____
_____
_____
_____
_____
_____
_____
_____

○ _____
○ _____
○ _____
○ _____
○ _____
○ _____
○ _____
○ _____
○ _____

21 FRIDAY

_____
_____
_____
_____
_____
_____
_____
_____
_____
_____
_____
_____
_____
_____
_____
_____
_____
_____

○ _____
○ _____
○ _____
○ _____
○ _____
○ _____
○ _____
○ _____
○ _____

22 SATURDAY

_____
_____
_____
_____
_____
_____
○ _____
○ _____
○ _____
○ _____

23 SUNDAY

_____
_____
_____
_____
_____
_____
_____
○ _____
○ _____
○ _____
○ _____

Notes and shit

_____
_____
_____

June 2024

24 MONDAY

25 TUESDAY

26 WEDNESDAY

○
○
○
○
○
○
○
○
○

○
○
○
○
○
○
○
○
○

○
○
○
○
○
○
○
○
○

Important as fuck

Fucking grateful for...

May your bucket list be as long as your fuck it list

27 THURSDAY

_____
_____
_____
_____
_____
_____
_____
_____
_____
_____
_____
_____
_____
_____
_____
_____
_____
○ _____
○ _____
○ _____
○ _____
○ _____
○ _____
○ _____
○ _____
○ _____

28 FRIDAY

_____
_____
_____
_____
_____
_____
_____
_____
_____
_____
_____
_____
_____
_____
_____
_____
_____
○ _____
○ _____
○ _____
○ _____
○ _____
○ _____
○ _____
○ _____
○ _____

29 SATURDAY

_____
_____
_____
_____
_____
_____
○ _____
○ _____
○ _____
○ _____

30 SUNDAY

_____
_____
_____
_____
_____
_____
○ _____
○ _____
○ _____
○ _____

Notes and shit

_____
_____
_____

July 2024

Sunday	Monday	Tuesday	Wednesday
	1 Canada Day (CA)	2	3
7	8 Muharram	9	10
14	15	16	17
21	22	23	24
28	29	30	31

Fuckity fuck fuck. Mean people suck.

Thursday	Friday	Saturday	Important shit
4 Independence Day (US)	5	6	_____ _____ _____ _____
11	12	13	_____ _____ _____ _____
18	19	20	_____ _____ _____
25	26	27	_____ _____ _____ _____
			_____ _____ _____ _____

June 2024

S	M	T	W	T	F	S
						1
2	3	4	5	6	7	8
9	10	11	12	13	14	15
16	17	18	19	20	21	22
23	24	25	26	27	28	29
30						

August 2024

S	M	T	W	T	F	S
				1	2	3
4	5	6	7	8	9	10
11	12	13	14	15	16	17
18	19	20	21	22	23	24
25	26	27	28	29	30	31

July 2024

1 MONDAY

Canada Day (CA)

_____
_____
_____
_____
_____
_____
_____
_____
_____
_____
_____
_____
_____
_____
_____
_____
_____

- ○ _____
- ○ _____
- ○ _____
- ○ _____
- ○ _____
- ○ _____
- ○ _____
- ○ _____
- ○ _____

2 TUESDAY

_____
_____
_____
_____
_____
_____
_____
_____
_____
_____
_____
_____
_____
_____
_____
_____
_____

- ○ _____
- ○ _____
- ○ _____
- ○ _____
- ○ _____
- ○ _____
- ○ _____
- ○ _____
- ○ _____

3 WEDNESDAY

_____
_____
_____
_____
_____
_____
_____
_____
_____
_____
_____
_____
_____
_____
_____
_____
_____

- ○ _____
- ○ _____
- ○ _____
- ○ _____
- ○ _____
- ○ _____
- ○ _____
- ○ _____
- ○ _____

Important as fuck

_____
_____
_____

Fucking grateful for...

_____
_____
_____

Even in the summer, you are chill as fuck

4 THURSDAY

Independence Day (US)

_____
_____
_____
_____
_____
_____
_____
_____
_____
_____
_____
_____
_____
_____
_____
_____
_____
_____

O _____
O _____
O _____
O _____
O _____
O _____
O _____
O _____
O _____

5 FRIDAY

_____
_____
_____
_____
_____
_____
_____
_____
_____
_____
_____
_____
_____
_____
_____
_____
_____
_____

O _____
O _____
O _____
O _____
O _____
O _____
O _____
O _____
O _____

6 SATURDAY

_____
_____
_____
_____
_____
_____
O _____
O _____
O _____
O _____

7 SUNDAY

_____
_____
_____
_____
_____
O _____
O _____
O _____
O _____

Notes and shit

_____
_____
_____

July 2024

_____

_____

_____

_____

_____

_____

_____

_____

_____

_____

_____

_____

_____

_____

_____

_____

_____

_____

○ _____

○ _____

○ _____

○ _____

○ _____

○ _____

○ _____

○ _____

○ _____

Important as fuck

_____

_____

Fucking grateful for...

_____

_____

Good morning, badass. Will you be operating in light mode or dark mode today?

11 THURSDAY

_____
_____
_____
_____
_____
_____
_____
_____
_____
_____
_____
_____
_____
_____
_____
_____
_____

○ _____
○ _____
○ _____
○ _____
○ _____
○ _____
○ _____
○ _____
○ _____

12 FRIDAY

_____
_____
_____
_____
_____
_____
_____
_____
_____
_____
_____
_____
_____
_____
_____
_____
_____

○ _____
○ _____
○ _____
○ _____
○ _____
○ _____
○ _____
○ _____
○ _____

13 SATURDAY

_____
_____
_____
_____
_____
○ _____
○ _____
○ _____
○ _____

14 SUNDAY

_____
_____
_____
_____
_____
○ _____
○ _____
○ _____
○ _____

Notes and shit

_____
_____
_____

July 2024

15 MONDAY

16 TUESDAY

17 WEDNESDAY

Important as fuck

Fucking grateful for...

love the fuck out of yourself

18 THURSDAY

_____
_____
_____
_____
_____
_____
_____
_____
_____
_____
_____
_____
_____
_____
_____
_____

○ _____
○ _____
○ _____
○ _____
○ _____
○ _____
○ _____
○ _____
○ _____

19 FRIDAY

_____
_____
_____
_____
_____
_____
_____
_____
_____
_____
_____
_____
_____
_____
_____
_____

○ _____
○ _____
○ _____
○ _____
○ _____
○ _____
○ _____
○ _____
○ _____

20 SATURDAY

_____
_____
_____
_____
_____
_____
○ _____
○ _____
○ _____
○ _____

21 SUNDAY

_____
_____
_____
_____
_____
_____
_____
○ _____
○ _____
○ _____
○ _____

Notes and shit

_____
_____
_____

July 2024

○
○
○
○
○
○
○
○
○

Important as fuck

Fucking grateful for...

Swearing is caring. Which basically makes you Mother Fucking Teresa.

25 THURSDAY

_____
_____
_____
_____
_____
_____
_____
_____
_____
_____
_____
_____
_____
_____
_____

○ _____
○ _____
○ _____
○ _____
○ _____
○ _____
○ _____
○ _____
○ _____

26 FRIDAY

_____
_____
_____
_____
_____
_____
_____
_____
_____
_____
_____
_____
_____
_____

○ _____
○ _____
○ _____
○ _____
○ _____
○ _____
○ _____
○ _____
○ _____

27 SATURDAY

_____
_____
_____
_____
_____
_____
○ _____
○ _____
○ _____
○ _____

28 SUNDAY

_____
_____
_____
_____
_____
_____
_____
○ _____
○ _____
○ _____
○ _____

Notes and shit

_____
_____
_____

July-August 2024

29 MONDAY   **30 TUESDAY**   **31 WEDNESDAY**

Important as fuck

Fucking grateful for...

You are bullshit proof

1 THURSDAY

_____
_____
_____
_____
_____
_____
_____
_____
_____
_____
_____
_____
_____
_____
_____
_____
_____
○ _____
○ _____
○ _____
○ _____
○ _____
○ _____
○ _____
○ _____
○ _____

2 FRIDAY

_____
_____
_____
_____
_____
_____
_____
_____
_____
_____
_____
_____
_____
_____
_____
_____
_____
○ _____
○ _____
○ _____
○ _____
○ _____
○ _____
○ _____
○ _____
○ _____

3 SATURDAY

_____
_____
_____
_____
_____
_____
○ _____
○ _____
○ _____
○ _____

4 SUNDAY

_____
_____
_____
_____
_____
_____
○ _____
○ _____
○ _____
○ _____

Notes and shit

_____
_____
_____

August 2024

Sunday	Monday	Tuesday	Wednesday
4	5 Civic Holidays (CA)	6	7
11	12	13	14
18	19	20	21
25	26 Summer Bank Holiday (UK)	27	28

Hot mess? I prefer sizzling chaos.

Thursday	Friday	Saturday	Important shit
1	2	3	_____
8	9	10	_____
15	16	17	_____
22	23	24	_____
29	30	31	_____

July 2024

S	M	T	W	T	F	S
	1	2	3	4	5	6
7	8	9	10	11	12	13
14	15	16	17	18	19	20
21	22	23	24	25	26	27
28	29	30	31			

September 2024

S	M	T	W	T	F	S
1	2	3	4	5	6	7
8	9	10	11	12	13	14
15	16	17	18	19	20	21
22	23	24	25	26	27	28
29	30					

August 2024

○
○
○
○
○
○
○
○
○

○
○
○
○
○
○
○
○
○

○
○
○
○
○
○
○
○
○

Important as fuck

Fucking grateful for...

Some days you just have to drop a few f-bombs and blow some shit up

8 THURSDAY

_____
_____
_____
_____
_____
_____
_____
_____
_____
_____
_____
_____
_____
_____
_____
_____

○ _____
○ _____
○ _____
○ _____
○ _____
○ _____
○ _____
○ _____
○ _____

9 FRIDAY

_____
_____
_____
_____
_____
_____
_____
_____
_____
_____
_____
_____
_____
_____

○ _____
○ _____
○ _____
○ _____
○ _____
○ _____
○ _____
○ _____
○ _____

10 SATURDAY

_____
_____
_____
_____
_____
_____
○ _____
○ _____
○ _____
○ _____

11 SUNDAY

_____
_____
_____
_____
_____
_____
○ _____
○ _____
○ _____
○ _____

Notes and shit

_____
_____
_____

August 2024

12 MONDAY

13 TUESDAY

14 WEDNESDAY

○
○
○
○
○
○
○
○
○

Important as fuck

Fucking grateful for...

When your brilliance throws a glare on your screen #Awesomebitchproblems

15 THURSDAY

_____
_____
_____
_____
_____
_____
_____
_____
_____
_____
_____
_____
_____
_____
_____

○ _____
○ _____
○ _____
○ _____
○ _____
○ _____
○ _____
○ _____
○ _____

16 FRIDAY

_____
_____
_____
_____
_____
_____
_____
_____
_____
_____
_____
_____
_____
_____
_____

○ _____
○ _____
○ _____
○ _____
○ _____
○ _____
○ _____
○ _____
○ _____

17 SATURDAY

_____
_____
_____
_____
_____
_____
○ _____
○ _____
○ _____
○ _____

18 SUNDAY

_____
_____
_____
_____
_____
_____
_____
○ _____
○ _____
○ _____
○ _____

Notes and shit

_____
_____
_____

August 2024

○
○
○
○
○
○
○
○
○

Important as fuck

Fucking grateful for...

Sometimes practicing gratitude sounds like, "Thanks a lot motherfucker."

22 THURSDAY

_____
_____
_____
_____
_____
_____
_____
_____
_____
_____
_____
_____
_____
_____
_____
_____
_____
○ _____
○ _____
○ _____
○ _____
○ _____
○ _____
○ _____
○ _____
○ _____

23 FRIDAY

_____
_____
_____
_____
_____
_____
_____
_____
_____
_____
_____
_____
_____
_____
_____
_____
_____
○ _____
○ _____
○ _____
○ _____
○ _____
○ _____
○ _____
○ _____
○ _____

24 SATURDAY

_____
_____
_____
_____
_____
_____
○ _____
○ _____
○ _____
○ _____

25 SUNDAY

_____
_____
_____
_____
_____
_____
_____
○ _____
○ _____
○ _____
○ _____

Notes and shit

_____
_____
_____

August-September 2024

Important as fuck

Fucking grateful for...

Dear Aliens, We're totally cool with you abducting assholes

29 THURSDAY

_____
_____
_____
_____
_____
_____
_____
_____
_____
_____
_____
_____
_____
_____
_____
_____
_____

○ _____
○ _____
○ _____
○ _____
○ _____
○ _____
○ _____
○ _____
○ _____

30 FRIDAY

_____
_____
_____
_____
_____
_____
_____
_____
_____
_____
_____
_____
_____
_____
_____
_____
_____

○ _____
○ _____
○ _____
○ _____
○ _____
○ _____
○ _____
○ _____
○ _____

31 SATURDAY

_____
_____
_____
_____
_____
_____

○ _____
○ _____
○ _____
○ _____

1 SUNDAY

_____
_____
_____
_____
_____
_____

○ _____
○ _____
○ _____
○ _____

Notes and shit

_____
_____
_____

September 2024

Sunday	Monday	Tuesday	Wednesday
1	2 Labor Day (US, CA)	3	4
8	9	10	11
15	16	17	18
22 Fall begins	23	24	25
29	30		

Do your best and fuck the rest

Thursday	Friday	Saturday	Important shit
5	6	7	_____
			_____
12	13	14	_____
19	20	21	_____
26	27	28	_____
			_____

September 2024

Important as fuck

Fucking grateful for...

Attention all Mondays. Assholery will no longer be tolerated. ~Fucking Management

5 THURSDAY

_____
_____
_____
_____
_____
_____
_____
_____
_____
_____
_____
_____
_____
_____
_____
_____
- ○ _____
- ○ _____
- ○ _____
- ○ _____
- ○ _____
- ○ _____
- ○ _____
- ○ _____
- ○ _____

6 FRIDAY

_____
_____
_____
_____
_____
_____
_____
_____
_____
_____
_____
_____
_____
- ○ _____
- ○ _____
- ○ _____
- ○ _____
- ○ _____
- ○ _____
- ○ _____
- ○ _____
- ○ _____

7 SATURDAY

_____
_____
_____
_____
_____
- ○ _____
- ○ _____
- ○ _____
- ○ _____

8 SUNDAY

_____
_____
_____
_____
_____
_____
_____
- ○ _____
- ○ _____
- ○ _____
- ○ _____

Notes and shit

_____
_____
_____

September 2024

9 MONDAY

10 TUESDAY

11 WEDNESDAY

○ _____
○ _____
○ _____
○ _____
○ _____
○ _____
○ _____
○ _____
○ _____

○ _____
○ _____
○ _____
○ _____
○ _____
○ _____
○ _____
○ _____
○ _____

○ _____
○ _____
○ _____
○ _____
○ _____
○ _____
○ _____
○ _____
○ _____

Important as fuck

Fucking grateful for...

Don't let a shitty day trick you into thinking you have a shitty life

12 THURSDAY

_____
_____
_____
_____
_____
_____
_____
_____
_____
_____
_____
_____
_____
_____
_____
_____

○ _____
○ _____
○ _____
○ _____
○ _____
○ _____
○ _____
○ _____
○ _____

13 FRIDAY

_____
_____
_____
_____
_____
_____
_____
_____
_____
_____
_____
_____
_____

○ _____
○ _____
○ _____
○ _____
○ _____
○ _____
○ _____
○ _____
○ _____

14 SATURDAY

_____
_____
_____
_____
_____

○ _____
○ _____
○ _____
○ _____

15 SUNDAY

_____
_____
_____
_____
_____
_____

○ _____
○ _____
○ _____
○ _____

Notes and shit

_____
_____
_____

September 2024

16 MONDAY

17 TUESDAY

18 WEDNESDAY

○
○
○
○
○
○
○
○
○

Important as fuck

Fucking grateful for...

If you wouldn't say it to a friend, don't say it to yourself, bitch. ~Your Sweary Godmother

19 THURSDAY

_____
_____
_____
_____
_____
_____
_____
_____
_____
_____
_____
_____
_____
_____
_____
_____
_____
_____

○ _____
○ _____
○ _____
○ _____
○ _____
○ _____
○ _____
○ _____
○ _____

20 FRIDAY

_____
_____
_____
_____
_____
_____
_____
_____
_____
_____
_____
_____
_____
_____
_____
_____
_____
_____

○ _____
○ _____
○ _____
○ _____
○ _____
○ _____
○ _____
○ _____
○ _____

21 SATURDAY

_____
_____
_____
_____
_____
_____
_____
○ _____
○ _____
○ _____
○ _____

22 SUNDAY
Fall begins

_____
_____
_____
_____
_____
_____
_____

○ _____
○ _____
○ _____
○ _____

Notes and shit

_____
_____
_____

September 2024

Important as fuck

Fucking grateful for...

Anything is possible with a little sunshine and swearing

26 THURSDAY

_____
_____
_____
_____
_____
_____
_____
_____
_____
_____
_____
_____
_____
_____
_____
_____

○ _____
○ _____
○ _____
○ _____
○ _____
○ _____
○ _____
○ _____
○ _____

27 FRIDAY

_____
_____
_____
_____
_____
_____
_____
_____
_____
_____
_____
_____
_____
_____

○ _____
○ _____
○ _____
○ _____
○ _____
○ _____
○ _____
○ _____
○ _____

28 SATURDAY

_____
_____
_____
_____
_____
○ _____
○ _____
○ _____
○ _____

29 SUNDAY

_____
_____
_____
_____
_____
_____
○ _____
○ _____
○ _____
○ _____

Notes and shit

_____
_____
_____

September-October 2024

Rosh Hashana begins at sundown

○
○
○
○
○
○
○
○
○

Important as fuck

Fucking grateful for...

What doesn't kill you, makes you stronger. Guess you're pretty ripped by now ;)

3 THURSDAY

_____
_____
_____
_____
_____
_____
_____
_____
_____
_____
_____
_____
_____
_____
_____
_____

○ _____
○ _____
○ _____
○ _____
○ _____
○ _____
○ _____
○ _____
○ _____

4 FRIDAY

_____
_____
_____
_____
_____
_____
_____
_____
_____
_____
_____
_____
_____
_____
_____
_____

○ _____
○ _____
○ _____
○ _____
○ _____
○ _____
○ _____
○ _____
○ _____

5 SATURDAY

_____
_____
_____
_____
_____
_____
○ _____
○ _____
○ _____
○ _____

6 SUNDAY

_____
_____
_____
_____
_____
_____
_____
○ _____
○ _____
○ _____
○ _____

Notes and shit

_____
_____
_____

October 2024

Sunday	Monday	Tuesday	Wednesday
		1	2 Rosh Hashana begins at sundown
6	7	8	9
13	14 Columbus Day (US), Thanksgiving (CA)	15	16
20	21	22	23
27 Daylight Saving Time ends (UK)	28	29	30

Time to get hygge AF

Thursday	Friday	Saturday
3	4	5
10	11 Yom Kippur begins at sundown	12
17	18	19
24	25	26
31 Halloween		

Important shit

_____
_____
_____
_____
_____
_____
_____
_____
_____
_____
_____
_____
_____
_____
_____
_____
_____
_____
_____
_____
_____
_____
_____
_____
_____
_____
_____

September 2024

S	M	T	W	T	F	S
1	2	3	4	5	6	7
8	9	10	11	12	13	14
15	16	17	18	19	20	21
22	23	24	25	26	27	28
29	30					

November 2024

S	M	T	W	T	F	S
					1	2
3	4	5	6	7	8	9
10	11	12	13	14	15	16
17	18	19	20	21	22	23
24	25	26	27	28	29	30

October 2024

7 MONDAY

8 TUESDAY

9 WEDNESDAY

Important as fuck

Fucking grateful for...

A fuck-up is not the end of the world. More like the start of a good story.

10 THURSDAY

_____
_____
_____
_____
_____
_____
_____
_____
_____
_____
_____
_____
_____
_____
_____
_____
_____
_____
_____

O _____
O _____
O _____
O _____
O _____
O _____
O _____
O _____
O _____

11 FRIDAY

Yom Kippur begins at sundown

_____
_____
_____
_____
_____
_____
_____
_____
_____
_____
_____
_____
_____
_____
_____
_____
_____

O _____
O _____
O _____
O _____
O _____
O _____
O _____
O _____
O _____

12 SATURDAY

_____
_____
_____
_____
_____
O _____
O _____
O _____
O _____

13 SUNDAY

_____
_____
_____
_____
_____
_____
_____
_____
O _____
O _____
O _____
O _____

Notes and shit

_____
_____
_____

October 2024

Columbus Day (US), Thanksgiving (CA)

○
○
○
○
○
○
○
○
○

Important as fuck

Fucking grateful for...

Happy Fucking New Week! Just a reminder that you can try new stuff any time you want. Not just January.

17 THURSDAY

18 FRIDAY

19 SATURDAY

○
○
○
○

20 SUNDAY

○
○
○
○
○
○
○
○
○

○
○
○
○
○
○
○
○
○

○
○
○
○

Notes and shit

October 2024

21 MONDAY

22 TUESDAY

23 WEDNESDAY

○
○
○
○
○
○
○
○
○

Important as fuck

Fucking grateful for...

Float like a butterfly, sting like a bee. If you swear like a sailor, sit next to me.

24 THURSDAY

_____
_____
_____
_____
_____
_____
_____
_____
_____
_____
_____
_____
_____
_____

○ _____
○ _____
○ _____
○ _____
○ _____
○ _____
○ _____
○ _____
○ _____

25 FRIDAY

_____
_____
_____
_____
_____
_____
_____
_____
_____
_____
_____
_____
_____
_____

○ _____
○ _____
○ _____
○ _____
○ _____
○ _____
○ _____
○ _____
○ _____

26 SATURDAY

_____
_____
_____
_____
_____

○ _____
○ _____
○ _____
○ _____

27 SUNDAY
Daylight Saving Time ends (UK)

_____
_____
_____
_____

○ _____
○ _____
○ _____
○ _____

Notes and shit

_____
_____
_____

October-November 2024

Important as fuck

Fucking grateful for...

Hey CAPTCHA, enough screening for robots. Start screening out assholes.

31 THURSDAY
Halloween

_____
_____
_____
_____
_____
_____
_____
_____
_____
_____
_____
_____
_____
_____
_____
_____
_____

O _____
O _____
O _____
O _____
O _____
O _____
O _____
O _____
O _____

1 FRIDAY
Diwali

_____
_____
_____
_____
_____
_____
_____
_____
_____
_____
_____
_____
_____
_____
_____
_____
_____

O _____
O _____
O _____
O _____
O _____
O _____
O _____
O _____
O _____

2 SATURDAY

_____
_____
_____
_____
_____
_____

O _____
O _____
O _____
O _____

3 SUNDAY
Daylight Saving Time ends (US, CA)

_____
_____
_____
_____
_____
_____

O _____
O _____
O _____
O _____

Notes and shit

_____
_____
_____

November 2024

Sunday	Monday	Tuesday	Wednesday
3 Daylight Saving Time ends (US, CA)	4	5 Election Day (US), Guy Fawkes Day (UK)	6
10 Remebrance Sunday (UK)	11 Veterans Day (US), Remebrance Day (CA)	12	13
17	18	19	20
24	25	26	27

Stick up for yourself. That's what middle fingers are for.

Thursday	Friday	Saturday	Important shit
	1 Diwali	2	_____
7	8	9	_____
14	15	16	_____
21	22	23	_____
28 Thanksgiving Day (US)	29	30	_____

October 2024

S	M	T	W	T	F	S
		1	2	3	4	5
6	7	8	9	10	11	12
13	14	15	16	17	18	19
20	21	22	23	24	25	26
27	28	29	30	31		

December 2024

S	M	T	W	T	F	S
1	2	3	4	5	6	7
8	9	10	11	12	13	14
15	16	17	18	19	20	21
22	23	24	25	26	27	28
29	30	31				

November 2024

4 MONDAY

5 TUESDAY

Election Day (US), Guy Fawkes Day (UK)

6 WEDNESDAY

○
○
○
○
○
○
○
○
○

Important as fuck

Fucking grateful for...

Forgive the sports analogy, but grab today by the balls

7 THURSDAY

8 FRIDAY

9 SATURDAY

○
○
○
○

10 SUNDAY
Remembrance Sunday (UK)

○
○
○
○
○
○
○
○
○

○
○
○
○
○
○
○
○
○

○
○
○
○

Notes and shit

November 2024

11 MONDAY
Veterans Day (US), Remembrance Day (CA)

12 TUESDAY

13 WEDNESDAY

Important as fuck

Fucking grateful for...

Failure is the only "F" word we should censor. It just means discovering ways that don't work. That's valuable fucking knowledge.

14 THURSDAY

_____
_____
_____
_____
_____
_____
_____
_____
_____
_____
_____
_____
_____
_____
_____
_____
_____
_____
_____
_____

○ _____
○ _____
○ _____
○ _____
○ _____
○ _____
○ _____
○ _____
○ _____

15 FRIDAY

_____
_____
_____
_____
_____
_____
_____
_____
_____
_____
_____
_____
_____
_____
_____
_____
_____

○ _____
○ _____
○ _____
○ _____
○ _____
○ _____
○ _____
○ _____
○ _____

16 SATURDAY

_____
_____
_____
_____
_____
○ _____
○ _____
○ _____
○ _____

17 SUNDAY

_____
_____
_____
_____
_____
_____
○ _____
○ _____
○ _____
○ _____

Notes and shit

_____
_____
_____

November 2024

18 MONDAY	19 TUESDAY	20 WEDNESDAY
_____	_____	_____
_____	_____	_____
_____	_____	_____
_____	_____	_____
_____	_____	_____
_____	_____	_____
_____	_____	_____
_____	_____	_____
_____	_____	_____
_____	_____	_____
_____	_____	_____
_____	_____	_____
_____	_____	_____
_____	_____	_____
_____	_____	_____
_____	_____	_____
_____	_____	_____
_____	_____	_____

○ _____ ○ _____ ○ _____
○ _____ ○ _____ ○ _____
○ _____ ○ _____ ○ _____
○ _____ ○ _____ ○ _____
○ _____ ○ _____ ○ _____
○ _____ ○ _____ ○ _____
○ _____ ○ _____ ○ _____
○ _____ ○ _____ ○ _____
○ _____ ○ _____ ○ _____

Important as fuck

Fucking grateful for...

You know what they say... a LOT of stupid shit you can ignore. You be you.

21 THURSDAY

_____
_____
_____
_____
_____
_____
_____
_____
_____
_____
_____
_____
_____
_____
_____
○ _____
○ _____
○ _____
○ _____
○ _____
○ _____
○ _____
○ _____
○ _____

22 FRIDAY

_____
_____
_____
_____
_____
_____
_____
_____
_____
_____
_____
_____
_____
_____
_____
○ _____
○ _____
○ _____
○ _____
○ _____
○ _____
○ _____
○ _____
○ _____

23 SATURDAY

_____
_____
_____
_____
_____
○ _____
○ _____
○ _____
○ _____

24 SUNDAY

_____
_____
_____
_____
_____
_____
○ _____
○ _____
○ _____
○ _____

Notes and shit

_____
_____
_____

November–December 2024

25 MONDAY

26 TUESDAY

27 WEDNESDAY

Important as fuck

Fucking grateful for...

Take a deep breath and imagine that another badass bitch is giving thanks for you.
Because they are.

28 THURSDAY

Thanksgiving Day (US)

_____
_____
_____
_____
_____
_____
_____
_____
_____
_____
_____
_____
_____
_____
_____
_____
_____

○ _____
○ _____
○ _____
○ _____
○ _____
○ _____
○ _____
○ _____
○ _____

29 FRIDAY

_____
_____
_____
_____
_____
_____
_____
_____
_____
_____
_____
_____
_____
_____
_____

○ _____
○ _____
○ _____
○ _____
○ _____
○ _____
○ _____
○ _____
○ _____

30 SATURDAY

_____
_____
_____
_____
_____
_____
○ _____
○ _____
○ _____
○ _____

1 SUNDAY

_____
_____
_____
_____
_____

○ _____
○ _____
○ _____
○ _____

Notes and shit

_____
_____
_____

December 2024

Sunday	Monday	Tuesday	Wednesday
1	2	3	4
8	9	10	11
15	16	17	18
22	23	24 Christmas Eve	25 Christmas Day, Hanukkah begins at sundown
29	30	31 New Year's Eve	

You're not naughty. You're just coal-oriented.

Thursday	Friday	Saturday	Important shit
5	6	7	_____
			_____
			_____
12	13	14	_____
			_____
19	20	21	_____
		Winter begins	_____
26	27	28	_____
Boxing Day (UK, CA), Kwanzaa begins (US, CA)			_____
			_____

November 2024

S	M	T	W	T	F	S
					1	2
3	4	5	6	7	8	9
10	11	12	13	14	15	16
17	18	19	20	21	22	23
24	25	26	27	28	29	30

January 2025

S	M	T	W	T	F	S
			1	2	3	4
5	6	7	8	9	10	11
12	13	14	15	16	17	18
19	20	21	22	23	24	25
26	27	28	29	30	31	

December 2024

Important as fuck

Fucking grateful for...

Be kind. Unless someone is being an asshole. Then, be kind of bitchy.

5 THURSDAY

6 FRIDAY

7 SATURDAY

- O
- O
- O
- O

8 SUNDAY

5 THURSDAY
- O
- O
- O
- O
- O
- O
- O
- O
- O

6 FRIDAY
- O
- O
- O
- O
- O
- O
- O
- O
- O

7 / 8
- O
- O
- O
- O

Notes and shit

December 2024

9 MONDAY

10 TUESDAY

11 WEDNESDAY

○
○
○
○
○
○
○
○
○

Important as fuck

Fucking grateful for...

Are you tired of hearing "You are enough"? Tough titties. Because you are always enough. Abso-fucking-lutely.

12 THURSDAY

13 FRIDAY

14 SATURDAY

- ○
- ○
- ○
- ○

15 SUNDAY

○
○
○
○
○
○
○
○
○

○
○
○
○
○
○
○
○
○

○
○
○
○

Notes and shit

December 2024

16 MONDAY   **17 TUESDAY**   **18 WEDNESDAY**

Important as fuck

Fucking grateful for...

You don't swear at the top of your lungs. You perform.

19 THURSDAY

_____
_____
_____
_____
_____
_____
_____
_____
_____
_____
_____
_____
_____
_____
_____
_____
_____

○ _____
○ _____
○ _____
○ _____
○ _____
○ _____
○ _____
○ _____
○ _____

20 FRIDAY

_____
_____
_____
_____
_____
_____
_____
_____
_____
_____
_____
_____
_____
_____
_____
_____

○ _____
○ _____
○ _____
○ _____
○ _____
○ _____
○ _____
○ _____
○ _____

21 SATURDAY

Winter begins

_____
_____
_____
_____
_____
○ _____
○ _____
○ _____
○ _____

22 SUNDAY

_____
_____
_____
_____
_____
_____
○ _____
○ _____
○ _____
○ _____

Notes and shit

_____
_____
_____

December 2024

23 MONDAY

24 TUESDAY

Christmas Eve

25 WEDNESDAY

Christmas Day, Hanukkah begins at sundown

- ○
- ○
- ○
- ○
- ○
- ○
- ○
- ○
- ○

- ○
- ○
- ○
- ○
- ○
- ○
- ○
- ○
- ○

- ○
- ○
- ○
- ○
- ○
- ○
- ○
- ○
- ○

Important as fuck

Fucking grateful for...

Finish on a fucking high note

26 THURSDAY

Boxing Day (UK, CA), Kwanzaa begins (US, CA)

- _____
- _____
- _____
- _____
- _____
- _____
- _____
- _____
- _____
- _____
- _____
- _____

○ _____
○ _____
○ _____
○ _____
○ _____
○ _____
○ _____
○ _____
○ _____

27 FRIDAY

- _____
- _____
- _____
- _____
- _____
- _____
- _____
- _____
- _____
- _____
- _____

○ _____
○ _____
○ _____
○ _____
○ _____
○ _____
○ _____
○ _____
○ _____

28 SATURDAY

- _____
- _____
- _____
- _____
- _____

○ _____
○ _____
○ _____
○ _____

29 SUNDAY

- _____
- _____
- _____
- _____
- _____

○ _____
○ _____
○ _____
○ _____

Notes and shit

_____
_____
_____

December 2024-January 2025

30 MONDAY

31 TUESDAY

New Year's Eve

1 WEDNESDAY

New Year's Day

○
○
○
○
○
○
○
○
○

○
○
○
○
○
○
○
○
○

○
○
○
○
○
○
○
○
○

Important as fuck

Fucking grateful for...

Great news: 2025 is also Year of the Badass. ♥

My Brilliant Thoughts & Shit

My Brilliant Thoughts & Shit

My Brilliant Thoughts & Shit

My Brilliant Thoughts & Shit

THANK YOU FOR CHOOSING
SASSY QUOTES PRESS

Here is your bonus gift!

For *instant access* to your
48 Sweary Affirmation Cards
color printables, please visit
www.sassyquotespress.com/bonus
No email signup required!

A favor please

Would you take a quick minute to leave this book a
rating/review on Amazon?
It makes a HUGE difference, and I would really appreciate it!
Thank you!

Jen @ Sassy Quotes Press

IMPORTANT: If the book you received was not printed correctly or was damaged during shipping, ***please return to Amazon for a perfectly printed copy or a refund***. I fucking hate when that happens! Amazon does a great job printing and shipping books, but errors do happen occasionally. Thank you for understanding!

More Fun From Sassy Quotes Press

Check out our hilarious planners, coloring books
and gratitude journals with lots of sweary quotes inside.

Visit
amazon.com/author/sassyquotespress

Or scan this QR code with your device

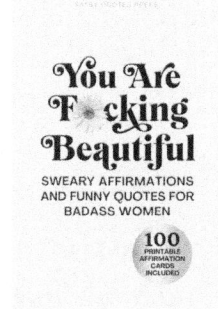

Printed in Great Britain
by Amazon

35148883R00084